all you need is love

LIZZIE CORNWALL

summersdale

ALL YOU NEED IS LOVE

First published in 2011

This edition copyright © Summersdale Publishers Ltd, 2017

Summersdale Publishers Ltd
46 West Street
Chichester
West Sussex
PO19 1RP
UK

www.summersdale.com

Printed and bound in Croatia

ISBN: 978-1-84953-970-8

Substantial discounts on bulk quantities of Summersdale books are available to corporations, professional associations and other organisations. For details contact general enquiries: telephone: +44 (0) 1243 771107, fax: +44 (0) 1243 786300 or email: enquiries@summersdale.com.

TO:............................

FROM:........................

The best thing to
hold onto in life
is each other.

Audrey Hepburn

WHAT THE WORLD REALLY
NEEDS IS MORE LOVE AND
LESS PAPERWORK.

Pearl Bailey

THE MORE I THINK IT OVER,
THE MORE I FEEL THAT
THERE IS NOTHING MORE
TRULY ARTISTIC THAN TO
LOVE PEOPLE.

Vincent Van Gogh

I AM IN LOVE —
AND, MY GOD, IT'S THE
GREATEST THING THAT CAN
HAPPEN TO A MAN.

D. H. Lawrence

THE WAR BETWEEN THE
SEXES IS THE ONLY ONE
IN WHICH BOTH SIDES
REGULARLY SLEEP WITH
THE ENEMY.

Quentin Crisp

WHERE THERE IS LOVE
THERE IS NO QUESTION.

Albert Einstein

IF GRASS CAN GROW
THROUGH CEMENT, LOVE
CAN FIND YOU AT EVERY
TIME IN YOUR LIFE.

Cher

Every time
we love, every
time we give,
it's Christmas.

DALE EVANS

IT WAS NOT MY
LIPS YOU KISSED,
BUT MY SOUL.

Judy Garland

IN THE SPRING A YOUNG
MAN'S FANCY LIGHTLY TURNS
TO THOUGHTS OF LOVE.

Alfred, Lord Tennyson

THE WORLD NEEDS
MORE LOVE AT
FIRST SIGHT.

Maggie Stiefvater

In love
the paradox
occurs that
two beings
become one
and yet
remain two.

ERICH FROMM

Eventually you will come to understand that love heals everything, and love is all there is.

Gary Zukav

A KISS IS A LOVELY TRICK
DESIGNED BY NATURE TO
STOP SPEECH WHEN WORDS
BECOME SUPERFLUOUS.

Ingrid Bergman

LOVE'S LIKE THE MEASLES —
ALL THE WORSE WHEN IT
COMES LATE IN LIFE.

Douglas Jerrold

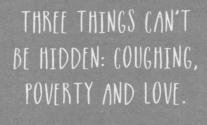

THREE THINGS CAN'T
BE HIDDEN: COUGHING,
POVERTY AND LOVE.

Yiddish proverb

SOMETIMES THE HEART
SEES WHAT IS INVISIBLE
TO THE EYE.

H. Jackson Brown Jr

LOVE IS LIKE SMILING;
IT NEVER FADES AND
IS CONTAGIOUS.

Paula Deen

ANYONE CAN BE PASSIONATE,
BUT IT TAKES REAL LOVERS
TO BE SILLY.

Rose Franken

To fall in love
you have to be
in the state
of mind for it
to take, like
a disease.

NANCY MITFORD

IT IS IMPOSSIBLE TO LOVE AND BE WISE.

Francis Bacon

LOVE IS NOT THE DYING
MOAN OF A DISTANT VIOLIN
— IT'S THE TRIUMPHANT
TWANG OF A BEDSPRING.

S. J. Perelman

I MARRIED THE FIRST MAN
I EVER KISSED. WHEN I TELL
THIS TO MY CHILDREN, THEY
JUST ABOUT THROW UP.

Barbara Bush

Love is an irresistible desire to be irresistibly desired.

ROBERT FROST

There is only one happiness in life: to love and be loved.

George Sand

NEVER GO TO BED MAD.
STAY UP AND FIGHT.

Phyllis Diller

A MAN IS ALREADY
HALFWAY IN LOVE WITH
ANY WOMAN WHO LISTENS
TO HIM.

Brendan Francis

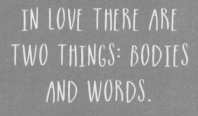

IN LOVE THERE ARE
TWO THINGS: BODIES
AND WORDS.

Joyce Carol Oates

LOVE IS A GRAVE
MENTAL DISEASE.

Plato

LOVE IS THE CONDITION
IN WHICH THE HAPPINESS
OF ANOTHER PERSON IS
ESSENTIAL TO YOUR OWN.

Robert A. Heinlein

DO YOU WANT ME TO TELL
YOU SOMETHING REALLY
SUBVERSIVE? LOVE IS
EVERYTHING IT'S
CRACKED UP TO BE.

Erica Jong

A heart
that loves
is always
young.

GREEK PROVERB

MY HEART IS EVER AT YOUR SERVICE.

William Shakespeare

ROMANCE IS THINKING
ABOUT YOUR SIGNIFICANT
OTHER, WHEN YOU ARE
SUPPOSED TO BE THINKING
ABOUT SOMETHING ELSE.

Nicholas Sparks

I HAVE SPREAD MY DREAMS
UNDER YOUR FEET; TREAD
SOFTLY BECAUSE YOU TREAD
ON MY DREAMS.

W. B. Yeats

To be in love is merely to be in a state of perpetual anaesthesia.

H. L. MENCKEN

Friendship in marriage is the spark that lights an everlasting flame.

Fawn Weaver

LOVE DOES NOT CONSIST
IN GAZING AT EACH OTHER,
BUT IN LOOKING OUTWARD
TOGETHER IN THE SAME
DIRECTION.

Antoine de Saint-Exupéry

LOVE IS BLIND —
MARRIAGE IS THE
EYE-OPENER.

Pauline Thomason

HAVE A HEART THAT NEVER
HARDENS, AND A TEMPER
THAT NEVER TIRES, AND A
TOUCH THAT NEVER HURTS.

Charles Dickens

IF YOU REALLY LOVE
SOMEONE AND CARE ABOUT
HIM, YOU CAN SURVIVE
MANY DIFFICULTIES.

Calvin Klein

LOVE CAN TURN THE COTTAGE
INTO A GOLDEN PALACE.

German proverb

ROMANCE CANNOT
BE PUT INTO QUANTITY
PRODUCTION — THE MOMENT
LOVE BECOMES CASUAL, IT
BECOMES COMMONPLACE.

Frederick Lewis Allen

Ultimately love is everything.

M. SCOTT PECK

FALLING IN LOVE CONSISTS MERELY IN UNCORKING THE IMAGINATION AND BOTTLING THE COMMON SENSE.

Helen Rowland

LOVE IS LIKE DEW
THAT FALLS ON BOTH
NETTLES AND LILIES.

Swedish proverb

WHAT WOULD MEN BE
WITHOUT WOMEN? SCARCE,
SIR, MIGHTY SCARCE.

Mark Twain

No more thou, and no more I, We, and only we!

RICHARD MONCKTON MILNES

Love is not altogether
a delirium, yet it
has many points in
common therewith.

Thomas Carlyle

WHAT FORCE IS MORE
POTENT THAN LOVE?

Igor Stravinsky

HE IS NOT A LOVER WHO
DOES NOT LOVE FOREVER.

Euripides

LOVE IS NOT CONSOLATION,
IT IS LIGHT.

Simone Weil

YOU KNOW YOU'RE IN LOVE
WHEN YOU CAN'T FALL ASLEEP
BECAUSE REALITY IS FINALLY
BETTER THAN YOUR DREAMS.

Anonymous

THERE IS TIME FOR WORK.
AND TIME FOR LOVE. THAT
LEAVES NO OTHER TIME.

Coco Chanel

TO FALL IN LOVE IS TO
CREATE A RELIGION THAT
HAS A FALLIBLE GOD.

Jorge Luis Borges

Where love is concerned, too much is not even enough.

PIERRE DE BEAUMARCHAIS

LOVE IS THE
MAGICIAN THAT
PULLS MAN OUT
OF HIS OWN HAT.

Ben Hecht

THERE IS NO HEAVEN
LIKE MUTUAL LOVE.

George Granville

YOU COME TO LOVE
NOT BY FINDING THE
PERFECT PERSON, BUT
BY LEARNING TO SEE
AN IMPERFECT PERSON
PERFECTLY.

Sam Keen

A life without love is like a year without summer.

SWEDISH PROVERB

Romance is everything.

Gertrude Stein

LOVE HAS NO UTTERMOST, AS
THE STARS HAVE NO NUMBER
AND THE SEA NO REST.

Eleanor Farjeon

IF I KNOW WHAT LOVE IS,
IT IS BECAUSE OF YOU.

Hermann Hesse

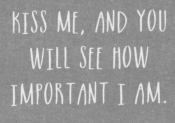

KISS ME, AND YOU
WILL SEE HOW
IMPORTANT I AM.

Sylvia Plath

TRUE LOVE COMES QUIETLY,
WITHOUT BANNERS OR
FLASHING LIGHTS. IF YOU
HEAR BELLS, GET YOUR
EARS CHECKED.

Erich Segal

A KISS THAT SPEAKS
VOLUMES IS SELDOM
A FIRST EDITION.

Clare Whiting

LOVE IS A FRIENDSHIP
SET TO MUSIC.

Joseph Campbell

Love is a
game that
two can play
and both win.

EVA GABOR

LOVE ISN'T
SOMETHING YOU
FIND. LOVE IS
SOMETHING THAT
FINDS YOU.

Loretta Young

MY WIFE ALWAYS SAID
A GOOD MEAL AND A GOOD
TANGO ARE ENOUGH TO MAKE
YOU HAPPY. SHE'S RIGHT.

Robert Duvall

IT'S LOVE THAT BRINGS
PEOPLE CLOSER.

Sunita Choudhary

I've been married so long I'm on my third bottle of Tabasco sauce.

SUSAN VASS

Talk not of wasted affection; affection never was wasted.

Henry Wadsworth Longfellow

LOVE RECOGNISES NO
BARRIERS. IT JUMPS
HURDLES, LEAPS FENCES,
PENETRATES WALLS
TO ARRIVE AT ITS
DESTINATION FULL
OF HOPE.

Maya Angelou

THERE IS NEVER A TIME OR
A PLACE FOR TRUE LOVE.
IT HAPPENS ACCIDENTALLY,
IN A HEARTBEAT.

Sarah Dessen

TO LOVE AND WIN IS THE
BEST THING. TO LOVE AND
LOSE, THE NEXT BEST.

William Makepeace Thackeray

LOVE IS AN EXPLODING CIGAR
WE WILLINGLY SMOKE.

Lynda Barry

I LOVE HER AND THAT'S
THE BEGINNING OF
EVERYTHING.

F. Scott Fitzgerald

A MAN FALLS IN LOVE
THROUGH HIS EYES, A
WOMAN THROUGH HER EARS.

Woodrow Wyatt

A loving
heart is the
beginning of
all knowledge.

THOMAS CARLYLE

TO LOVE DEEPLY IN
ONE DIRECTION MAKES
US MORE LOVING IN
ALL OTHERS.

Sophie Swetchine

THE ART OF LOVE...
IS LARGELY THE ART
OF PERSISTENCE.

Albert Ellis

LOVE VANQUISHES TIME.

Mary Parrish

Love is not consolation. It is light.

FRIEDRICH NIETZSCHE

You have made a place in my heart where I thought there was no room for anything else.

Robert Jordan

NO JOB IS AS IMPORTANT
TO ME AS MY LOVE.

Jennifer Aniston

IT'S EASY TO FALL IN LOVE.
THE HARD PART IS FINDING
SOMEONE TO CATCH YOU.

Bertrand Russell

STRONG WOMEN LEAVE
BIG HICKIES.

Madonna

LOVE IS FRIENDSHIP
SET ON FIRE.

Jeremy Taylor

LUST IS EASY.
LOVE IS HARD. LIKE IS
MOST IMPORTANT.

Carl Reiner

IF I HAD A FLOWER
FOR EVERY TIME
I THOUGHT OF YOU... I
COULD WALK THROUGH
MY GARDEN FOREVER.

Alfred, Lord Tennyson

When I saw
you I fell in
love. And you
smiled because
you knew.

ARRIGO BOITO

WHATEVER OUR
SOULS ARE MADE OF,
HIS AND MINE ARE
THE SAME.

Emily Brontë

LOVE IS THE JOY OF THE
GOOD, THE WONDER OF THE
WISE, THE AMAZEMENT
OF THE GODS.

Plato

SOUL MEETS SOUL
ON LOVERS' LIPS.

Percy Bysshe Shelley

Each moment
of a happy
lover's hour is
worth an age
of dull and
common life.

APHRA BEHN

You don't love someone because they're perfect, you love them in spite of the fact they're not.

Jodi Picoult

AND YET, TO SAY THE
TRUTH, REASON AND LOVE
KEEP LITTLE COMPANY
TOGETHER NOWADAYS.

William Shakespeare

LOVE CONQUERS ALL THINGS;
LET US TOO SURRENDER
TO LOVE.

Virgil

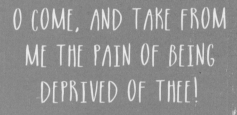

O COME, AND TAKE FROM
ME THE PAIN OF BEING
DEPRIVED OF THEE!

Thomas Campion

LOVE AND WAR ARE
THE SAME THING, AND
STRATAGEMS AND POLICY
ARE AS ALLOWABLE IN THE
ONE AS IN THE OTHER.

Miguel de Cervantes

THE WORLD IS TOO
DANGEROUS FOR ANYTHING
BUT TRUTH AND TOO SMALL
FOR ANYTHING BUT LOVE.

William Sloane Coffin

I REALLY THINK THAT ALL MEN SHOULD CELEBRATE THEIR WOMEN... THEY SHOULD ALL JUMP ON COUCHES FOR THEM.

Tom Cruise

Everything is clearer when you're in love.

JOHN LENNON

ONE DOES NOT FALL
'IN' OR 'OUT' OF
LOVE. ONE GROWS
IN LOVE.

Leo Buscaglia

YOU CAN'T PUT A PRICE TAG
ON LOVE, BUT YOU CAN ON
ALL ITS ACCESSORIES.

Melanie Clark

LOVE IS AN INDESCRIBABLE
SENSATION — PERHAPS A
CONVICTION, A SENSE
OF CERTITUDE.

Joyce Carol Oates

Laugh and the world laughs with you, snore and you sleep alone.

ANTHONY BURGESS

She knew she loved him when 'home' went from being a place to being a person.

E. Leventhal

NO LOVE IS ENTIRELY
WITHOUT WORTH, EVEN
WHEN THE FRIVOLOUS CALLS
TO THE FRIVOLOUS AND THE
BASE TO THE BASE.

Iris Murdoch

TO GET THE FULL
VALUE OF JOY YOU
MUST HAVE SOMEONE
TO DIVIDE IT WITH.

Mark Twain

ONE OF THE SECRETS OF LIFE
IS THAT ALL THAT IS REALLY
WORTH THE DOING IS WHAT
WE DO FOR OTHERS.

Lewis Carroll

TO FIND SOMEONE THAT
WILL LOVE YOU FOR NO
REASON... THAT IS THE
ULTIMATE HAPPINESS.

Robert Brault

WHEN WE ARE IN LOVE WE
SEEM TO OURSELVES QUITE
DIFFERENT FROM WHAT
WE WERE BEFORE.

Blaise Pascal

MY WIFE AND I TRIED
TO BREAKFAST TOGETHER,
BUT WE HAD TO STOP OR
OUR MARRIAGE WOULD
HAVE BEEN WRECKED.

Winston Churchill

Love is
composed of
a single soul
inhabiting
two bodies.

ARISTOTLE

WE ARE SHAPED AND FASHIONED BY THOSE WE LOVE.

Johann Wolfgang von Goethe

THE BEST WAY TO GET
HUSBANDS TO DO SOMETHING
IS TO SUGGEST THAT... THEY
ARE TOO OLD TO DO IT.

Shirley MacLaine

ONE WORD FREES US OF ALL
THE WEIGHT AND PAIN OF
LIFE: THAT WORD IS LOVE.

Sophocles

Marriage is a very good thing, but I think it's a mistake to make a habit out of it.

W. SOMERSET MAUGHAM

The only thing
worse than a man
you can't control is
a man you can.

Margo Kaufman

LOVE IS BEING STUPID TOGETHER.

Paul Valéry

KISS ME AND YOU
WILL SEE HOW
IMPORTANT I AM.

Sylvia Plath

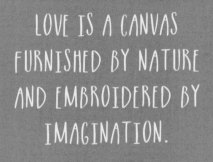

LOVE IS A CANVAS
FURNISHED BY NATURE
AND EMBROIDERED BY
IMAGINATION.

Voltaire

I FELL IN LOVE THE WAY
YOU SLEEP: SLOWLY, AND
THEN ALL AT ONCE.

John Green

YOUR WORDS ARE MY FOOD,
YOUR BREATH MY WINE. YOU
ARE EVERYTHING TO ME.

Sarah Bernhardt

DON'T LET LOVE INTERFERE
WITH YOUR APPETITE. IT
NEVER DOES WITH MINE.

Anthony Trollope

Love at first sight? I absolutely believe in it! You've got to keep the faith.

LEONARDO DICAPRIO

NEXT TO BEING
MARRIED, A GIRL
LIKES TO BE CROSSED
IN LOVE A LITTLE
NOW AND THEN.

Jane Austen

TROUBLE IS, BY THE TIME
YOU CAN READ A GIRL LIKE
A BOOK, YOUR LIBRARY
CARD HAS EXPIRED.

Milton Berle

LOVE IS AN ELECTRIC
BLANKET WITH SOMEBODY
ELSE IN CONTROL OF
THE SWITCH.

Cathy Carlyle

I want to
do with
you what
spring does
with cherry
trees.

PABLO NERUDA

Marriage is a dinner that begins with dessert.

Henri de Toulouse-Lautrec

LOVE IS BUT THE DISCOVERY
OF OURSELVES IN OTHERS,
AND THE DELIGHT IN
THE RECOGNITION.

Alexander Smith

IN YOUR LIGHT I LEARN
HOW TO LOVE.

Rumi

WHO, BEING LOVED,
IS POOR?

Oscar Wilde

ROMANCE IS THE GLAMOUR
WHICH TURNS THE DUST
OF EVERYDAY INTO
A GOLDEN HAZE.

Elinor Glyn

TO LOVE IS TO RECEIVE A
GLIMPSE OF HEAVEN.

Karen Sunde

LOVE CONQUERS ALL
THINGS EXCEPT POVERTY
AND TOOTHACHE.

Mae West

'Tis better to
have loved
and lost
Than never
to have
loved at all.

ALFRED, LORD TENNYSON

NOBODY HAS EVER
MEASURED, NOT EVEN
POETS, HOW MUCH
THE HEART CAN HOLD.

Zelda Fitzgerald

TRUST YOUR HEART IF THE
SEAS CATCH FIRE, LIVE BY
LOVE THOUGH THE STARS
WALK BACKWARD.

E. E. Cummings

LOVE KNOWS NOT DISTANCE;
IT HATH NO CONTINENT; ITS
EYES ARE FOR THE STARS.

Gilbert Parker

All love is original, no matter how many other people have loved before.

GEORGE WEINBERG

The winds were warm about us, the whole earth seemed the wealthier for our love.

Harriet Elizabeth Prescott Spoffor

TO LOVE IS TO FEEL ONE
BEING IN THE WORLD AT
ONE WITH US, OUR EQUAL IN
SIN AS WELL AS IN VIRTUE.

Emmuska Orczy

I HAVE GREAT HOPES
THAT WE SHALL LOVE EACH
OTHER ALL OUR LIVES AS
MUCH AS IF WE HAD NEVER
MARRIED AT ALL.

Lord Byron

WE LOVE BECAUSE IT'S THE
ONLY TRUE ADVENTURE.

Nikki Giovanni

LOVE IS LIKE PI —
NATURAL, IRRATIONAL AND
VERY IMPORTANT.

Lisa Hoffman

AS THE ARTERIES
GROW HARD, THE HEART
GROWS SOFT.

H. L. Mencken

MARRIAGE MAY OFTEN BE A
STORMY LAKE, BUT CELIBACY
IS ALMOST ALWAYS A
MUDDY HORSEPOND.

Thomas Love Peacock

To love and be loved is to feel the sun from both sides.

DAVID VISCOTT

LIFE WITHOUT LOVE IS LIKE A TREE WITHOUT BLOSSOMS OR FRUIT.

Kahlil Gibran

THE MAGIC OF FIRST LOVE
IS OUR IGNORANCE THAT IT
CAN EVER END.

Benjamin Disraeli

LOVE DOES NOT ALTER THE
BELOVED, IT ALTERS ITSELF.

Søren Kierkegaard

Real love stories never have endings.

RICHARD BACH

IF YOU'RE INTERESTED IN FINDING OUT MORE ABOUT OUR BOOKS, FIND US ON FACEBOOK AT SUMMERSDALE PUBLISHERS AND FOLLOW US ON TWITTER AT @SUMMERSDALE.

www.summersdale.com